Overcoming Depression

Bob Gass

Overcoming Depression

Healing for Your Mind and Emotions

Bob Gass
with
Ruth Gass-Halliday

Overcoming Depression:
Healing for Your Mind and Emotions

ISBN: 978-1-93172-718-0 (hard back)
ISBN: 978-1-4507-3324-3 (paper back)

Post Office Box 5130, Alpharetta, Georgia 30023

Pray about everything.
Tell God what you need, and thank him
for all he has done. If you do this,
you will experience God's peace,
which is far more wonderful
than the human mind can understand.
His peace will guard your hearts and minds
as you live in Christ Jesus.

PHILIPPIANS 4:6-7 NLT

Contents

"Most of us can talk openly about the illnesses of our bodies, but when it comes to illnesses of the mind we clam up. And because we do, people with emotional disorders feel ashamed, stigmatized, and don't seek the help that can make a difference."

Actor Kirk Douglas

CHAPTER ONE

The 12-Foot Cage

The story is told of a zoo in Europe that purchased a big brown bear from a traveling circus. All its life the bear had been cooped up in an iron cage 12 feet long. Every waking hour, with its massive head swaying rhythmically from side to side, it paced out the dimensions of that cage—12 feet forward and 12 feet back.

The people who came to see it were both curious and cruel. Some would toss cigarette butts into its cage to burn the pads of its feet and break the march. One man fed it hamburger meat laced with glass slivers and it hemorrhaged until the blood ran down to its haunches. But it survived, to keep on doing what it did best, marching—12 feet forward and 12 feet back.

But a new day dawned for the big brown bear. It was about to be transferred to a beautiful zoo. Now in this particular zoo bears didn't live in cages, they lived on boundless acres of plush, carpet-like green grass. There were tall-limbed trees lazy bears could sleep under and energetic ones could climb. There were sparkling pools of water to drink from and splash in. There were three square meals a day guaranteed. And best of all, there were other bears for fun and fellowship.

So the zoo keepers wheeled the big iron cage out onto the compound, opened the door, and what do you think happened? Nothing! Oblivious to the open door and the call to a larger life he just kept on marching—12 feet forward and 12 feet back.

They called to the bear but he wouldn't come out. They offered him freedom, food, and the fellowship of other bears, but he didn't respond. Finally, to get him out of his cage, they put a burning kerosene-soaked rag on the end of a long pole and prodded it through the bars. Intimidated by the smell of smoke and the sight of fire the big bear jumped out of his cage onto the grass. But was he free? No! As they watched in amazement he began to pace the exact dimensions of his old psychological captivity—12 feet forward and 12 feet back.

At that moment it dawned on them that his prison was not *metal,* it was *mental.* The bars may as well have been made of straw as of steel; it made no difference. His prison was in his mind!

After exhausting every remedy they knew, they released the big brown bear through the only door left—they put him to sleep in death.

The story captured the interest of people everywhere. On a television talk show a panel of experts discussed what more they could have done. Finally one spoke up and said, "You could have taken that bear to the vast Alaskan wilderness with its salmon-filled rivers and endless miles of forest and that wouldn't have been reality to him. Reality to him was only one thing—12 feet forward and 12 feet back.

This book is for those who live in a 12-foot cage called depression! It's also for those who long to help them.

For some it's a gilded cage in an affluent suburb; for others it's a blue-collar cage in a run-down part of town. It makes no difference. The steps are always the same—12 feet forward and 12 feet back.

But there's a way out! Jesus said He came to "proclaim freedom to those who are held captive" and "to release the oppressed."

And that's what this book is all about!

*"Fits of depression come over most of us.
The strong are not always vigorous, the wise not
always ready, the brave not always courageous,
and the joyous not always happy.
There may be here and there men of iron...
but surely the rust frets even these."*

CHARLES SPURGEON

CHAPTER TWO

A Common Enemy

Depression is often referred to as "the common cold" of the counselor's office. It can stem from the death of a loved one, prolonged illness, guilt, resentment, financial problems, stress, relationship difficulties or heredity.

Unlike feeling blue for a few days, depression can persist for months or years. Its symptoms include: sadness, hopelessness, a sense of worthlessness, constant anxiety, learned helplessness, and lack of interest in socializing and other activities that were once sources of enjoyment. Some other symptoms are fatigue; loss of interest in sexual intimacy; difficulty concentrating, remembering and making decisions; insomnia and oversleeping; overeating and under eating; suicidal thoughts;

restlessness, anger and irritability; and persistent vague physical problems like headaches and stomachaches that don't respond to treatment.

Here's how some of those affected describe it:

"I feel worthless, like I haven't accomplished what I should; yet I don't have the energy. I'm disconnected from the people in my life, even friends and family who care about me. I don't want to get out of bed and I'm losing hope that life will ever get better."

"My days are dark and gloomy. The air feels dense, like I can't breathe. I'm paralyzed by fear and insecurity. I just want to hide and not have to face the world. My work performance is going downhill. My whole life seems to be in a tailspin."

"My husband doesn't understand. He just wants me to 'get over it.' My kids keep asking why I'm always in hiding and feel so sad. I've been struggling with suicidal thoughts for several weeks. I just can't bear the pain and confusion any longer."

So, what should you do when you or someone you love is in the grip of depression? Talk to your doctor! Jesus said, "Healthy people don't need a doctor, but sick people do" (Mt 9:12 CEV). Just as your mind affects your body, your body affects your mind. Your doctor is trained to diagnose and treat physical imbalances and deficiencies. He can also refer you to a specialist. There are different types of depression: some respond to counseling and therapy, others require safe, effective and proven medications. Don't self-medicate. What works for somebody else may actually make you feel worse.

Too many of us have been shamed into thinking that asking for help and participating in any kind of therapy is a sign of weakness. One counselor writes: "Some of us have felt so alienated that we've forgotten we're not alone. We've come to believe that we have to do it ourselves. We've been abandoned, gone without love, gotten used to people never being there for us. But we *can* allow ourselves to be helped and supported. We *aren't* alone. And we *don't* have to do it ourselves."

The Bible strongly supports counseling: "Without good direction, people lose their way; the more wise counsel you follow, the better your chances" (Pr 11:14 TM). "To win, you need a lot of good counsel" (Pr 24:6 TM). In fact, one of the names given to Jesus is "Wonderful Counselor" (Is 9:6 NIV).

Just as a mirror lets you see your reflection, a good counselor can give you a clearer picture of yourself, outline your options, point you in the right direction, assure you that you're not unique and that things aren't hopeless, and help you regain control of your life.

Depression doesn't have to be a deadly downward spiral!

When Bethany Hamilton, once ranked as the best amateur teen surfer in Hawaii, lost her arm to a tiger shark, she'd every reason to be depressed. But she flat-out refused to give in to it. Instead she began to raise money to help a blind man. And on a visit to New York City she gave her ski jacket to a homeless girl. When somebody asked her about it, she replied, "I already have more than I need in life." Instead of throwing in the towel Bethany told her dad, "If having only one arm prevents me from being successful in competitive surfing then I'll see about playing soccer!" Today her compassion *and* competitiveness have reached new levels. Her pastor Steve Thompson says, "She's looking forward to the future, asking herself, 'How can I show the world I still have a life and that it's filled with joy?' She has an underlying trust that God is taking care of her." And she's not unique. The Bible's full of people who overcame depression and turned their pain into purpose:

(a) Jeremiah was so depressed he was ready to quit the ministry and go into the motel business! "O that I had in the wilderness a lodging place of wayfaring men; that I might leave my people" (Jer 9:2). Sickened by the moral and spiritual climate in the nation he declared, "[My grief is beyond healing], my heart is sick and faint within me!" (Jer 8:18 AMP). But he refused to let it immobilize him. Instead he took the focus off himself, began interceding with God and ended up bringing a spiritual awakening to his people.

(b) Nehemiah also experienced depression: "The city where my ancestors are buried is in ruins, and its gates have been burned down" (Ne 2:3 CEV). "When I heard...I sat down and wept" (Ne 1:4 NIV). But he didn't stay there long. His despondency motivated him to go back to Jerusalem and personally supervise the rebuilding of the city.

Henri Dunant, a wealthy 19th century Swiss banker, was sent to Paris by his government to work on a business deal with Napoleon. When he arrived he discovered that Napoleon was off fighting a war, so he went to the battlefront to find him. Once there, Dunant watched in horror as cannon balls ripped open human flesh. Maimed and dying men lay all around him. In fact he was so devastated by what he saw that he stayed at the front for weeks, helping doctors tend to the wounded.

After returning home Dunant was still haunted by those images. He couldn't keep his mind on banking and became so distracted that he lost his fortune. But even with his career in ruins he maintained a sense of God's sovereignty in all that had happened, and later wrote, "It seemed to me that I had something to accomplish, a sacred duty that was destined to have infinite consequence for mankind." And he was right. Out of depression and failure Henri Dunant went on to found the Red Cross, and for doing so received the first Nobel Peace Prize.

In the following chapters we'll look at *God's* prescription for dealing with depression and learn how we can fortify ourselves in the fight to overcome this common enemy.

"The greatest discovery of our generation
is that we can choose our attitude
in any given circumstance."

WILLIAM JAMES

CHAPTER THREE

"The Victim Trap"

One cold winter day a boy was walking home from school when he met a snake. "It's freezing out here, let me curl up inside your coat," the snake said. "No way," the boy exclaimed, "you'll only bite me!" The smooth-talking reptile assured him he'd never do that, so against his better judgment the boy tucked him inside his jacket and walked on. Well, you guessed it; the snake bit him. "But I trusted you!" the boy cried. "Why did you bite me?" Smiling, the snake replied, "You knew what I was when you picked me up, and I haven't changed!"

There are many causes for depression. One of them is *Satan*—and he hasn't changed either! "He has always been...a liar. There is nothing truthful about him" (Jn 8:44 CEV). Two of his favorite lies are "the forever lie," which tells you your situation will never change; and "the never lie," which says that even if things do change, you'll never be happy again. Both lies contradict God's Word. He says, "The plans I have for you...are plans for good" (Jer 29:11 NLT). Paul writes, "Even though on the outside it...looks like things are falling apart on us, on the inside...God is making new life" (2Co 4:16 TM).

The Apostle Peter warns: "That enemy of yours ...roams around like a lion...seeking someone to seize upon" (1Pe 5:8 AMP), and one of his most effective weapons is "The Victim Trap." He persuades you that nobody (not even God) understands how you feel. It's the oldest lie in the book, and once you buy into it you join the ranks of those who "awfulize" life and allow their problems to immobilize them.

During the good times it's easy to see God's hand at work. While Elijah was calling down fire from heaven, predicting the end of a drought, resurrecting a widow's son, outrunning a chariot and reprimanding an evil king, he never doubted for a second that God was with him. But as soon as Jezebel's death threats started, he fled for his life to the desert. Drained and depressed he plunked down under a tree and said, "I've had enough. Just let me die" (1Ki 19:4 CEV).

Anytime you feel like that, it's not from God!

Elijah was suffering from major burnout, so God drew him aside to rest and renew himself by spending time in His presence. Later we find the prophet depressed and in hiding again, this time in a cave. When God asks, "'What are you doing here, Elijah?' He replied, 'The Israelites have rejected your covenant, broken down your altars, and put your prophets to death with the sword. I am the only one left, and now they are trying to kill me too'" (1Ki 19:9-10 NIV). There's that old "victim" mentality at work again.

Elijah wasn't alone! God had seven thousand

others defending His cause throughout Israel. Elijah allowed his emotions to interpret the situation, and the moment his focus shifted from God to the enemy he was overwhelmed. Sound familiar?

Notice something: God didn't ask Elijah, "What are you doing *there?*" He asked, "What are you doing *here?*" (1Ki 19:9 TLB). Why did God phrase it like that? To let Elijah know *He* was in the cave along with him. And He's right beside you today too because that's the kind of God He is.

Look at David. For a long time it seemed like this man after God's own heart couldn't lose. Everything he touched turned to gold. Samuel anointed him king, he defeated Goliath, King Saul chose him as a warrior and musician, the army loved him and wrote songs about him.

It doesn't get much better!

Then he lost it all. His job and his marriage failed. Samuel, his old mentor, died. His best friend Jonathan couldn't help him. Saul's soldiers hounded him so hard that he fled for cover to the

Cave of Adullam.

It doesn't get much worse!

Eventually David came to the place where he could say of the Lord: "You are my only place of refuge" (Ps 142:5 TLB). Finding refuge in God means becoming so immersed in His Word, so hungry for His presence, so convinced of His goodness, so devoted to His Lordship, that wherever you are is fine—as long as *He's* there.

Jesus also understood loneliness. His life was in constant danger. For a while it seemed He'd lost His position as a leader and His status as a teacher. His friends deserted Him. Then He went to a cross and died. When He did, it seemed like His dreams, as well as those He'd inspired in others, died with Him.

Then His enemies put His body into a cave. A major mistake! They didn't know God does some of His best work in caves. It's where He resurrects dead things—like dead hopes, dead marriages, and dead self-worth.

Make no mistake, everybody does time in the cave. It's where you end up when your dreams are shattered, you've lost someone dear to you, your career is in ruins, your health is failing and your earthly supports are gone. And the hardest part of being there is fearing you'll never get out because God has forgotten you.

Jesus never promised smooth sailing. In fact, He said, "In this godless world you will (not probably or perhaps)...experience difficulties. But take heart! I've conquered the world" (Jn 16:33 TM). It's in the storms of life that you learn lessons you can't learn any other way. In situations you can't fix and can't escape, He introduces you to the meaning of grace and teaches you about trust and transcendent joy that lifts you above your circumstances.

If you're asking, "Lord, how much longer?" remember, when He doesn't deliver you immediately He'll be your thermostat in the fire. If He wasn't already regulating the heat you'd have burned up long ago, right? Every time you reached breaking point God put a "hold" on the enemy. He has the whole thing figured out and when it's over you're coming out of the fire like gold (See Job 23:10). You'll be refined, more valuable, and of greater use to Him and others.

And here are some things you'll learn in the process:

(1) To focus on God instead of your circumstances. Ever notice how cartoon characters can run off cliffs without falling and getting hurt? As long as they keep their legs pumping they can move faster in the air than on the ground. However, the moment they start to focus on their circumstances, they panic and plummet. Going over the cliff doesn't stop them—looking down does.

Matthew 14:30 says as soon as Peter "Looked ...at the...waves, he...began to sink" (TLB). As long as Peter was looking to Jesus the storm didn't matter, but as soon as he fixed his eyes on the waves, fear took him down. And it'll take *you* down, too!

By contrast, a shepherd boy named David heard about Goliath, a man so big he could easily have qualified for the World Wrestling Federation. Nobody would take him on. But David brought him down with a rag and a rock—because he tackled him in *God's* strength, not his own. That strategy still works!

The majority of Joshua's spies saw only giants: it's all they could talk about when they returned from the Promised Land. Consequently they spread depression throughout the ranks. As a result the Israelites gave in to fear and spent the next forty years in the wilderness, missing what God had for them. How different the outcome could have been if only they'd kept their focus on God's past faithfulness, obstacle-removing power and rock-solid promises.

Maybe you're asking God to lighten your burden and He wants to strengthen your back. Phyllis Michael writes:

What seems to be a stumbling block, may be
a stepping-stone;
What seems to be a solid wall, may be a
door unknown.
What seems to be a speck of dust, may be
in truth pure gold;
So walk by faith and not by sight, no good
will He withhold.

You can tell how strong you are by what it takes to discourage you. Sometimes our discouragement has nothing to do with what God does or doesn't do, and everything to do with our mistaken assumptions about how we *think* He should act. When we try to second-guess Him we're usually wrong, because He says, "I don't think the way you think" (Is 55:8 TM). God always has a plan, and His timing is perfect. In Genesis as Abraham was preparing to sacrifice Isaac, he "Looked up and saw a ram, caught...by its horns...and offered it...instead of his son" (Ge 22:13 NRS). Do you know what's interesting in this story? Rams don't normally climb that high—which proves that when God makes a promise to you, if He has to He'll break every natural law in the book to keep it. That's how it is with His provision. You don't usually see it coming or understand how He'll do it, but each step of faith brings you one step closer.

(2) That with God, sometimes words are unnecessary. One day a man overheard his little granddaughter repeating the alphabet. When he asked what she was doing she replied, "I'm praying, Grandpa, but I can't think of the right words. So I'm just saying all the letters and God can put them together 'cause He knows what I'm thinking." Paul says, "We don't even know what we should pray for...but the...Spirit [who lives within us] prays for us...And the Father...knows...what the Spirit is saying" (Ro 8:26-27 TLB). That means when you're so depressed you can't find words to pray, you can lift your heart to God, confident He understands what you need and will

provide it.

(3) That there's power in His Word. David said, "The precepts of the Lord are right, giving joy to the heart [and] giving light to the eyes" (Ps 19:8 NIV). Meditating on God's promises will decrease your depression and increase your joy. Maybe you think meditation is something only monks and mystics do, or people with too much time on their hands. If so, let me ask you: do you know how to worry? You do? Then you know how to meditate, because meditation is just thinking deeply and continuously about something, letting it simmer on the inside until it becomes part of you.

The point isn't how much Scripture you memorize but what happens to you in the process. Meditating on God's Word changes you by making you think *different* thoughts than if you were watching TV, out shopping at the mall, or obsessing on your problem. David said, "Your word I have hidden in my heart" (Ps 119:11 NKJV). When God's Word moves from your head to your heart, the results are attitude-altering and life-changing.

(4) How to monitor your self-talk! What you say limits or liberates you: "You are...snared by the words of your mouth" (Pr 6:2 NKJV). What you keep telling yourself eventually *becomes* your reality, so choose joy. Happiness usually depends on happenings, but joy is a choice; a choice based on what God says; a choice that empowers you to rise above the moment, the mood, the circumstance or the immediate outlook. Nehemiah said, "Be not...depressed...the joy of the Lord is your strength" (Ne 8:10 AMP). Joy is God's antidepressant. James wrote, "Consider it all joy (not just the parts you like!)...when you encounter... trials" (Jas 1:2 NAS). When the Psalmist says, "Joy comes in the morning" (Ps 30:5 NAS), that means it's waiting for you when you wake up. By deciding to walk in it regardless of the circumstances you face, you short-circuit Satan's plans for your day. In Ephesians 5:19, Paul says we do

this by speaking to one another in:

"Psalms." Max Lucado says, "Worship is the 'thank you' that refuses to be silenced; an act of gratitude offered by the saved to the Savior, the healed to the Healer, and the delivered to the Deliverer." Just as "Deep calleth unto deep" (Ps 42:7), Psalms encourage the kind of intimacy that creeps out of your spirit and into your worship.

"Hymns." Great hymns help you to break through the toughest of circumstances and emotions. They remind you of the truth of God's Word: "When peace like a river attendeth my way, When sorrows like sea billows roll, Whatever my lot, Thou hast taught me to say, 'it is well, it is well' with my soul."

"Spiritual songs." These are born out of the spontaneity of that moment when your heart overflows with love for God, and when He fills the screen of your mind, crowding everything else out.

"Making melody in our heart." This has nothing to do with your musical abilities. You can

have a singing heart even with your lips closed. It's the element that makes your eyes twinkle and your smile sparkle because this melody comes from the very depths of your being. The enemy may take everything else but never let him steal your singing heart. It may feel like midnight in a prison cell, but like Paul and Silas, with a singing heart you can break out and break through every time.

(5) That you choose the right response. Psychologist William James said: "The greatest discovery of our generation is that we can choose our attitude in any given circumstance." David said, "I *will* bless the Lord at all times: his praise *shall* continually be in my mouth" (Ps 34:1). Paul was in prison when he wrote, "Rejoice in the Lord always: and again I say, Rejoice" (Php 4:4).

Maybe you're depressed because your finances have taken a nose dive, the career you worked so hard to establish is floundering, or the people you trusted have disappointed you. When his life began to unravel the prophet Habakkuk wrote:

"Though the fig tree does not bud...there are no grapes on the vines...the olive crop fails...the fields produce no food...there are no sheep in the pen ...no cattle in the stalls, yet I will rejoice in the Lord" (Hab 3:17-18 NIV). This man recognized that while he couldn't control events, by God's grace he could control his attitude toward them. He chose to focus on the Lord, not the circumstances, and you must learn to do that too.

(6) How to walk in God's strength, not your own. The Bible says, "He gives power to the faint, and strengthens the powerless" (Isa 40:29 NRS). One day as Professor James Loder of Princeton Theological Seminary was traveling with his wife Arlene, they stopped to help two ladies fix a flat tire. As he knelt to work another driver rammed their car, pushing it on top of him. Loder writes:

"There was no one to help but my wife Arlene ...a slight woman barely over five feet tall. With her hands on the bumper she prayed, 'In the Name of Jesus Christ...in the Name of Jesus Christ.'

Recounting later, she said her strength began to give way and she lost consciousness for a few seconds. However, when she was able to refocus she was surprised to see that the car had been lifted! When Arlene Loder called on God that day He filled her with strength beyond imagination. As a result her husband's life was miraculously spared and his entire ministry changed.

David said, "Blessed is the man whose strength is in thee" (Ps 84:5), because when you draw on *God's* strength you accomplish things you never thought possible!

"Grant me the enabling grace to believe
without feeling, to know without seeing,
to clasp your invisible hand
and wait with trust for the morning."

Ruth Harms-Calkin

CHAPTER FOUR

God Cares

Ever notice when you're feeling down, well-meaning friends telling you to cheer up just makes you feel worse? Why? Because it invalidates your emotions and confirms that they really don't understand.

Some people think Christians aren't supposed to get depressed; it must mean we don't have enough faith or that there's hidden sin in our lives. Depression doesn't discriminate! Those who battle this silent enemy are all around us—including some of our best-known leaders and ministers. The reason we can't hear them is because their cries have been locked inside for years.

One woman battling depression described it as: "*Being trapped inside a cage so small that I can't stand up, can't move and can hardly breathe. This cage sits just outside the gates of hell. Even if there's a way out, it doesn't matter because I can't see it. Satan keeps promising me peace if I'll kill myself, and I'm starting to find his offer appealing."*

The Bible says, "A bruised reed he will not break" (Mt 12:20 NIV). What do you suppose all these people have in common: A guilt-ridden woman groveling before a religious mob ready to stone her; a quadriplegic on a cot begging his friends not to quit as they look at the crowd between them and Jesus; a blind beggar crying out for the Master's attention? They're all "bruised reeds" Jesus loved too much to pass by or give up on. And He won't give up on you either!

David said, "When my spirit was overwhelmed...You knew" (Ps 142:3 AMP). Jesus has a special place in his heart for those who are battling depression. He said, "If you are tired from carrying heavy burdens, come to me and I will give you rest" (Mt 11:28 CEV).

God never gives up on us—even when we give up on ourselves!

Peter said to Jesus, "We've worked hard all night and haven't caught anything" (Lk 5:5 NIV). Can't you hear the discouragement in his voice? Despite their skills as fishermen, the disciples kept coming up empty. However, everything changed when Jesus entered the picture and said: "Go out... deeper, and let down your nets" (Lk 5:4 NLT). When they obeyed a wonderful thing happened: "Their nets were so full they began to tear" (Lk 5:6 NLT).

Perhaps you're sitting today where Peter and the disciples sat. Your nets are empty, your future looks bleak and you're ready to give up. Jesus knows how hard you've tried, and today He invites you to go fishing again—this time with *Him*. If you've been wrestling with financial failure, tormenting memories, addiction, bitterness, marital problems, or health issues, don't jump ship! The Lord of second chances and new beginnings wants to come on board. He knows where the fish are biting because He put them there.

Jesus understands how you feel. "He had to enter into every detail of human life. Then, when he came before God as [our] high priest...he would have already experienced...all the pain, all the testing—and...be able to help" (Heb 2:17-18 TM). Jesus understands:

(a) Inferiority complexes. He grew up in a little backwater town among people who rejected Him. "He came to his own...but they didn't want him" (Jn 1:11 TM). His family said, "He's out of his mind" (Mk 3:21 NLT). When Philip told his brother, Nathanael, "'We've found the One Moses wrote of...Jesus...from Nazareth!' Nathanael replied, 'Nazareth...You've got to be kidding'" (Jn 1:45-46 TM). And Jesus' family tree was nothing to write home about either. Rahab was a prostitute, Jacob was a crook, David was an adulterer and a murderer—and you think *your* family is messed up!

(b) Feeling overwhelmed. "Crowds...were

coming and going so...Jesus...did not even have time to eat" (Mk 6:31 NCV). Not only did He have to cope with the endless needs of others, He had to constantly correct His own disciples who included uneducated fishermen, a religious bigot and a despised tax collector. How would you like to deal with that lot every day?

(c) Disappointment and betrayal. His friend Judas sold Him out to His enemies and sealed the deal with a kiss. And in the midst of His greatest trial His closest friends "Could not stay awake with [Him] for one hour" (Mt 26:40 NCV).

In Luke 4:1-2 we read, "Jesus...was led by the Spirit in the wilderness, where he was tempted by the devil" (NLT). You can have a "wilderness experience" anywhere: at a graveside, in an unemployment line, lying on a hospital bed or in the middle of a bitter divorce. It's the place where:

There's no end in sight and nobody to rescue you! It's a breeding ground for depression. It weakens your resolve and makes you vulnerable to temptation. A debilitating illness can tempt you to look for a quick way out. A troubled marriage can make you think "another" man or woman is the answer.

God tests your motives. Moses told the Israelites: "God led you...in the wilderness...to know what was in your heart, whether you would keep His commandments or not" (Dt 8:2 NKJV). God permits wilderness experiences to test our motives, correct our attitudes, and demonstrate His faithfulness.

Max Lucado wrote: "When we purchased a bike for five-year-old Jenna, three-year-old Andrea wanted one too. I explained that she was too young. No luck; she still wanted the bike. I explained when she got older she'd get one. She just stared at me. I told her a big bike would bring her more pain than pleasure, more scrapes than thrills. She just turned her head and said nothing. Finally, I told her daddy knew best. Her response? She screamed loud enough for everyone to hear, 'Then

I want a new daddy.' The words were from a child's mouth but they carried an adult's sentiment. Disappointment always demands a change in command. When we don't agree with the one calling the shots, our reaction is the same. With three-year-old logic Andrea couldn't believe a new bike could be anything less than ideal—a source of eternal bliss. And the one who could grant it was just sitting on his hands." Have you been feeling that way?

When you're in the wilderness you have two choices—withdraw from life and die inwardly. Or reach out to God and allow Him to use it for your good.

"As the eyes of servants look
to the hand of their masters...
so our eyes look to the Lord our God,
until He has mercy on us."

Psalm 123:2 NKJV

CHAPTER FIVE

Welcome to Life; Disappointment Guaranteed

Welcome to life; disappointment guaranteed! Webster defines disappointment as: "When expectations fail to be met, producing anger, frustration, sadness and discouragement." Here are five Scriptural examples to help you when:

(1) You're disappointed with those you look up to. Think of Samuel and Eli (See 1Sa 1-4). Samuel's mother entrusted her child to Eli the High Priest, confident he'd mentor and prepare him for God's service. But Eli had a serious character flaw. He was a weak, passive parent who stood by while his sons abused their priestly privilege, bringing shame and disrepute to the ministry. Who'd have blamed young Samuel for taking a

nose dive when the man he looked up to failed so badly? But no, he fielded his disappointment and kept his eyes and ears on God: "Samuel grew, and the Lord was with him" (1Sa 3:19). As a result God turned him into one of Israel's greatest prophets. So keep your eyes on the Lord.

(2) You're disappointed in those you live with. If anyone wouldn't let you down, surely it would be your family. Right? Wrong! Ask young Joseph. When God promised him a big promotion he thought his brothers would celebrate. Instead they responded with jealousy, ridicule and resentment, selling him into slavery. Far from friends and home he languished in prison for a crime he didn't commit. What an invitation to bitterness, to rehearsing the wrongs done him while plotting his revenge. But if he'd done that he'd have died an unknown convict in a foreign jail. Instead he allowed God to vindicate him, using his circumstances to position, prepare and promote him to being Egypt's Prime Minister.

(3) Disappointment in those you work with and depend on. To succeed, you need people; you can't make it without them. And when those people fail you it's painful. Imagine Moses' disappointment. He leaves his brother Aaron in charge while he attends a summit conference with God and receives the Ten Commandments. Returning, he finds Israel in anarchy, idolatry and unspeakable perversion. Where's Aaron? Leading the rebellion! When Moses needs him most, Aaron fails him miserably. But watch Moses; true leadership shines in deep disappointment. He confronts Aaron, takes the mess to God for resolution and prays forgiveness for Israel. God listens, then reminds Moses of his assignment. "[It's disappointing, Moses, but] 'go, lead the people...my angel will go before you'" (Ex 32:34 NIV). Disappointment doesn't cancel your assignment—or God's presence. Do what He sent you to do.

(4) Disappointment in those you've poured your life into. Let's check in again with Moses,

Founding Pastor of the First Church of the Critical and the Ungrateful, a congregation of former slaves, delivered, abundantly blessed, en route to the Promised Land, but without a shred of loyalty or gratitude for the man who put everything on the line to make it possible. Fresh out of Egypt they turn on Moses, accusing, blaming and berating him (See Ex 14). Was Moses disappointed and hurt? Yes. But each time he got fed up with their ingratitude and wanted to quit he'd discuss it with God, pray for his complaining flock, receive fresh orders from headquarters and return to work. It's what God-called men and women do when they're disappointed and feel like giving up.

(5) Disappointment in ourselves. It's potentially the most debilitating kind of disappointment because it can throw you into a downward spiral that's hard to stop or recover from.

Peter had sworn undying love and fidelity to Jesus. "Lord, everybody else may abandon you, but not me! I'm yours till death" (See Mt 26:33-75).

And he meant every word of it. But under the pressures surrounding the crucifixion he yielded, and three times denied knowing Jesus. Later, remembering Jesus' words, "Before the rooster crows, you'll deny me three times," Peter, heart-broken by his own dismal failure, "went outside and wept bitterly" (Lk 22:62 NIV). Ever asked, "God, how can you possibly use someone as messed up as me?" Peter failed to meet his own expectations and went on a downer. But Jesus wasn't shocked. He was well aware of Peter's flaws when he called him into the ministry. He also knew that his blustering, outspoken disciple had a tender heart, so He extended grace to him rather than remove him from office. When Christ gave post-resurrection orders to "tell His disciples and Peter" (Mk 16:7 NIV) to meet Him in Galilee, He reaffirmed His choice of the failed disciple. The rest of Peter's story is New Testament history.

When (not if!) you confront failure: (a) Don't add insult to injury by letting disappointment mire you in hopelessness and despair. (b) Humble yourself and repent. Confess your sin; don't excuse, rationalize or blame circumstances and people. (c) Receive God's grace and forgiveness by faith, not by feelings. Don't let Satan convince you your case is beyond grace. (d) Get whatever help you need to get back on track—sooner, not later.

Knowing you're accepted, valued and loved
by God, gives you the confidence
to stand up to the enemy.
It also allows you to stop working so hard
for other people's approval.

CHAPTER SIX

Are You a Target for Identity Theft?

During the 1920's a silent-movie star with fiery red hair and a heart-shaped face won the admiration of millions of moviegoers. Her name was Clara Bow. F. Scott Fitzgerald said of her, "This girl's the real thing, someone to stir every pulse." But even as the world sang her praises, behind the captivating smile and vivacious personality was a depressed, insecure young woman. Others may give you rave reviews but if inwardly you're filled with doubt and self-loathing, their praises will ring hollow.

Jesus said, "The thief comes...to steal" (Jn 10:10 NIV), and this thief doesn't want *just* your possessions, He wants something infinitely more valuable—your identity! He knows your self-worth is based on your self-perception.

Are you so obsessed with your inadequacies that you don't value your uniqueness? Are you so busy envying others that you can't appreciate what God's given you? Paul says we are not to "compare ourselves...as if one...were better and another worse ...Each of us is an original" (Gal 5:26 TM). Never give up who you are in order to become like somebody else. If two of us are identical, one of us is unnecessary. Glean what you can from everyone, but never try to duplicate them. Unfavorable comparisons imply that God made a mistake when He created you. Plus, it allows people to control you. By coveting what others have instead of developing your own talents, you set yourself up for disappointment and depression.

If you're struggling with insecurity and low self-esteem, praying longer, working harder and vowing to do better won't necessarily give you the results you want. Like remodeling a house with a cracked foundation, you can renovate from top to bottom but the floors and ceilings will just keep sagging till eventually the whole structure collapses. You must address the foundation—and you can only do that by knowing who you are in *God's* eyes. The Bible says, "Before he made the world... God...chose [you]" (Eph 1:4 NLT). Once you grasp that truth Satan can no longer diminish you. Knowing you're accepted, valued and loved by God gives you confidence to stand up to the enemy and lets you stop working so hard for other people's approval.

If you think that walking to a church altar to become a Christian means *you* chose the Lord—think again! Jesus said, "You didn't choose me. I chose you" (Jn 15:16 NLT), and He didn't do it based on your virtues. He chose and equipped you because He wants to fulfill His purposes through you. That's information Satan doesn't want you to have because it'll revolutionize your life.

We all want to be valued for who we are, and when we're not we use "things" to fill that void.

We seek fulfillment through endless activity, affairs, obsessing about our appearance or fixating on food or money. "Making the switch" involves: (a) recognizing the things and people from whom we draw our identity; (b) replacing old thought patterns with new ones; (c) accepting that our security and significance are wrapped up in our relationship with Jesus—and nothing else! God never created anything without value and purpose, including you. In His eyes you're:

Loved. The Bible says, "Nothing in all creation will ever...separate us from the love of God" (Ro 8:39 NLT). Did you get that? Nothing! God says, "I have loved you...with an everlasting love" (Jer 31:3 NLT). His love for you has no limits or expiration date.

Valued. "You are...God's own child...And... God has made you his heir" (Gal 4:7 NLT). You'll run out of needs before you'll exhaust God's supply. "Surely goodness and mercy shall follow me all the days of my life" (Ps 23:6).

Capable. Without a supportive home life it's easy to grow up with a diminished sense of worth and competency. But the Bible says, "God has given...you...special abilities" (1Pe 4:10 TLB), and it's your job to discover, develop and deploy them. Paul writes: "What you say about yourself means nothing...what God says...makes the difference" (2Co 10:18 TM). And what exactly is that? Well, for starters: He valued you enough to make you in His own image (See Ge 1:26-27). He fashioned your every detail with loving care (See Ps 139:13-16). He's always thinking about you (See Ps 139:1-3, 17). He wants to demonstrate His power through you (See 2Co 12:9). He thinks of you as His "special treasure" (See Dt 7:6 NLT). He promised never to leave or forsake you (See Mt 28:20). *That's* the on-the-record, morale-building opinion of the One whose opinion matters most, so don't allow Satan to steal your identity or let people make you feel "less than."

Paul says, "You are now fully adopted as his

own...an heir, with complete access to the inheritance" (Gal 4:5-7 TM). Notice the word "adopted." Sometimes parents have to make lifestyle changes to accommodate an unexpected pregnancy and raise an unplanned child. But nobody adopts by accident! With advance knowledge of your every weakness God chose you anyway. You were in His mind before you were in your mother's womb. Your parents didn't create you, He did. Do you realize the grace you walk under? You never have to worry about approaching your Father; you have a standing invitation. That's like having a platinum credit card; you get preferential treatment every time!

Paul says God is "sustaining all things by his powerful word" (Heb 1:3 NIV), and He won't speak something over your life, then stand back and watch it fall apart. He said, "My word... will...achieve the purpose for which I sent it" (Is 55:11 NIV).

Remember in Genesis when God said,

"Let there be lights in the...heavens to divide the day from the night" (Ge 1:14 NKJV)? That same sun and moon are still shining today, and the same Word that brought them into being still sustains them. Now, if God will do that for an inanimate planet, don't you think He'll do the same for *you?* Come on, start basing your self-esteem on the truth that God made you precisely, intricately, wondrously and uniquely who you are—a genuine one-off! Start accepting the truth, that He's transforming you daily into the person He wants you to become.

"People who soar are those who refuse to sit back, sigh, and wish things would change... They will not allow life's circumstances to push them down and hold them under."

Chuck Swindoll

CHAPTER SEVEN

Recognizing What Fuels Depression

Traveling through life at breakneck speed while ignoring your soul's warning lights, makes you a prime target for despair, self-condemnation and loneliness. Let's look at each.

Despair

Arthur Miller, who was married to Marilyn Monroe, tells of her descent into despondency. One evening after the doctor had given her yet another shot and she was sleeping, Miller stood watching her. "I found myself straining to imagine miracles," he writes. "What if she were to wake and I were able to say, 'God loves you, darling,' and she were able to believe it? How I wished I still had my religion and she hers."

In a research lab a dog lies motionless. Even when the electrified floor under him is turned on he makes no attempt to escape. He's hungry, but even hunger no longer motivates him. What's going on? Dr. Martin Seligman labeled it, "learned helplessness," and the explanation is simple enough. Involved in previous experiments, the dog learned that trying to escape was useless, and now, even though the situation has changed and he could easily get away, he passively accepts the pain.

Thankfully (for us and the dog) the condition is reversible. By forcing him to act, literally dragging him off the electrified floor, he eventually learns that responding *does* make a difference. But with some dogs it took as many as two-hundred-fifty attempts before they finally got it.

So is this some kind of new phenomenon? No. Solomon said, "I...gave my heart up to despair over all...my efforts" (Ecc 2:20 AMP). When your efforts seem futile, you feel isolated from God, and your heart protests. If you're not attuned to what it's saying, the next step is despair.

After four hundred years of slavery in Egypt God chose Moses to deliver His people, but "they refused to listen...because of their...anguish of spirit and... cruel bondage" (Ex 6:9 AMP). They'd experienced too much pain; they couldn't see beyond their immediate circumstances so they ended up settling for what the enemy handed out.

So did God give up on them? No, but He didn't instantly transport them to the Promised Land either. Instead of letting them slip quietly out of Egypt He multiplied "signs...wonders, and miracles" (Ex 7:3 AMP), to remind them again of His care and willingness to intervene on their behalf. And as if all those plagues weren't enough, God handed them the wealth of Egypt on their way to freedom!

They should have been happy campers, right? But they weren't. The next time the going got tough, instead of turning to the One who'd already proven Himself, they resorted to their old pattern of complaining and despair. Imagine: even though it meant hardship and slavery they were ready to return to Egypt and the comfort of the familiar! Like those laboratory dogs that repeatedly had to be pulled off the painful grid, the Israelites had to learn, and relearn to trust God regardless of the circumstances.

The Psalmist's despair was so severe that he asked God, "Why must I wander [in darkness]?... Why is my heart so sad? (Ps 42:9,11 NLT). Thankfully God doesn't just give us an account of David's dark days, He gives us the answer that David found. "You are my hiding place; you protect me from trouble. You surround me with songs of victory" (Ps 32:7 NLT).

When David's home in Ziklag was burned to the ground by his enemies, he could have said, "I guess I'll just have to settle for this." But instead he consulted God, and God said, "Go after them; you will recover everything that was taken" (1Sa 30:8 TLB). Re-read those words. "*You–will–recover.*" Write them down on a 3x5 card and carry it with you wherever you go! Each time you read them remind yourself, "I will recover because David's God is my God!" When David followed God's instructions he ended up rescuing his family and taking back his life. And with God's help you can too.

Taking action is powerful. A single step forward can rob hopelessness of its power. When Israel needed to cross the River Jordan God said, "Set foot in the Jordan...[and] its waters...will be cut off" (Jos 3:13 NIV). But first they had to leave the riverbank and step into the water. And the same goes for you.

Stop waiting for "the ideal moment," or for someone else to agree!

Roger Bannister, the first runner ever to break the four-minute mile, said, "Doctors and scientists said it was impossible, that one would die in the attempt. So when I got up from the track after collapsing at the finish line, I figured I was dead!"

Psychiatrist David Burns says: "When I'm

faced with a challenge and do nothing, it leads to distorted thoughts of helplessness. That, in turn, leads to loss of energy and motivation, damaged self-esteem and feeling overwhelmed. The end result is self-defeating behavior, and the whole cycle spirals downward."

Stop waiting for somebody to come and rescue you; God is calling *you* to act! Start where you are, not where you think you *should* be. Overcoming depression can begin by doing something as simple as: (1) Eating enough to fuel your body. As you become stronger physically you'll have more energy to tackle other areas. (2) Getting out of bed, showering, and taking a walk. Exercise stimulates and strengthens, and your goal is to become physically re-engaged in life. (3) Establishing a normal sleep pattern by getting up every morning at the same time and refusing to sleep until bedtime. No more retreating or hiding in sleep. Remember, the more areas of your life you reclaim the more you circumvent the cycle of despair.

Self-Condemnation

Forgiving others is central to overcoming depression. But there's more; unless you also learn to forgive yourself you'll go nowhere. Like driving a car with the brakes on, self-condemnation drags you down and steals your momentum. It also generates chemicals that increase your heart rate, raise your blood pressure, disrupt your digestion, tense your muscles, dump cholesterol into your bloodstream and reduce your ability to think clearly. Every time you revisit your "old issues" those bad feelings deliver another zap of corrosive chemicals. Today science confirms what God has always known. Namely, that people who can't forgive themselves are more prone to depression, heart attacks and other serious illnesses. To guard against this:

(1) Get rid of unrealistic expectations. We all have a set of subconscious rules about how we think we should behave. Many of them were formed in childhood and no longer work. For example, how realistic is it to think you can work

all day, accept every invitation, maintain a perfect house, get enough sleep, and still have time for God and yourself? No wonder His Word tells us to, "Look at the way we're living and reorder our lives" (La 3:40 TM).

(2) Learn to do good, instead of always feeling bad. The Bible says, "If you fail the test, do something about it" (2Co 13:5 TM). If you feel you failed as a parent, become a terrific grandparent. Get involved in something bigger than yourself. Longfellow said, "Give what you have. To someone it may be better than you think." What you do for yourself dies with you, what you do for others is timeless.

(3) Confess your mistakes. Psychologist Fred Luskin says it's particularly easy to berate yourself for failing at a major life task, like a marriage or career; or when your actions have hurt others, when your lifestyle choices have hurt you, or for not doing what you know you should. Confession is therapeutic; it stops you from slipping into denial. David

said, "When I kept it all inside...The pressure never let up...I said, 'I'll make a clean breast of my failures to God. Suddenly the pressure was gone—my guilt dissolved" (Ps 32:3-5 TM). Before David could move ahead he had to acknowledge his problem. That takes courage; especially when your first instinct is to bury it under a stoic exterior and pretend it never happened.

(4) Hit the "stop" button. Often the thing that's making you feel bad is not the offense itself, but the guilt associated with remembering what you did. Once you've repented and received God's forgiveness, the season for regret is over. (See Isa 43:25).

(5) Adopt the "Triple-A Formula." When a tragic accident left Will Mitchell with disfiguring burns, he focused on his possibilities instead of his problems. Although he'd lost his fingers he learned to fly an airplane solo. Then one day while flying from Colorado to California ice caused his plane to crash. Paralyzed from the waist down (and you

think *you've* got problems!) Mitchell was understandably depressed about being confined to a wheelchair for life. It was then that a friend gave him the same advice he'd earlier given her: "It doesn't matter what happens to you, what matters is what you decide to do about it." Mitchell adopted the Triple-A Formula: *Accept* what happens. *Appreciate* what you can learn from it. *Adapt* to the new opportunities it presents. Since then he's held public office, found love, and given hundreds of motivational talks. Mitchell says, "Before I was paralyzed there were ten thousand things I could do, now there are nine thousand. Should I focus on the one thousand I can't do? No, I'd rather concentrate on the nine thousand ways in which life's still good."

(6) Replace guilt with gratitude. Gratitude is a healing force, and finding things to be thankful for isn't difficult. Walk into any supermarket and thank God for the abundance of fresh food you enjoy. Visit a hospital and thank God for your

health. He gives us all 86,400 seconds every day. Use a few of them to say thank you and see the difference it makes in your outlook.

(7) Realize it's not just about you. By refusing to forgive yourself, you're making the decision to stay miserable. And misery loves company! When you beat yourself up, your loved ones get beaten up too. It's inevitable. When you wallow in guilt you're more withdrawn and critical, and less open and affectionate. That means your husband, wife, children, co-workers, friends—even your dog and cat—suffer along with you.

Loneliness

Today's rocketing suicide rates can be directly linked to loneliness and depression. Researcher René Spitz demonstrated that even when infants are routinely changed and fed, they fail to thrive unless they're also held and cuddled. Paul writes: "Do the hard work (yes, you have to work at it) of getting along with each other" (Jas 3:18 TM). As commendable as accomplishments are, they're no substitutes for relationships. History is filled with stories of people like Elvis Presley, Marilyn Monroe and Howard Hughes who accumulated wealth, fame and power, yet died lonely because they failed to connect with others on any meaningful level. The Bible says, "You belong in God's household" (Mk 8:38 CEV). Without a sense of belonging you're a candidate for depression. Next to your relationship with God what matters most is your connection to people. You need others to laugh, cry, love, grow old and die with.

Did you know that unlike creatures that travel in packs, porcupines travel solo? When they encounter other animals they respond by withdrawing and using their quills to attack. Once their deadly quills become embedded, the wounds fester causing suffering and even death. It's not that porcupines necessarily want to be alone, they just don't know how to get close without hurting others or themselves. Sound familiar? We employ attack-

and-withdrawal strategies every day. We have our own little set of quills, like gossip, anger, pride, competitiveness, insensitivity, greed and control. And by aiming them at people we damage relationships, hurt others and end up lonely.

The bottom line is this: while it's not always easy, porcupines need to be able to get along together to ensure future generations. Their only other option is extinction. So pull in your quills, and ask God to help you build loving relationships with the other porcupines who share your space!

This is not just a good idea, it's vital in overcoming depression!

"No man can live happily
who regards himself alone,
who turns everything to his own advantage.
You must live for others
if you wish to live for yourself."

Seneca, Roman Poet

CHAPTER EIGHT

The Recipe for Happiness

Often the things we hope will feed our souls, end up feeding our depression. Two of the most common things are:

(1) Thinking money buys happiness. It doesn't. The Bible says, "A bonanza at the beginning is no guarantee of blessing at the end" (Pr 20:21 TM). Regardless of how much you accumulate, it's never enough. Fear will always whisper that unless you acquire more, your survival is in danger. Solomon wrote, "He that loveth silver shall not be satisfied with silver; nor he that loveth abundance with increase" (Ecc 5:10). Logan Pearsall Smith says, "There are two things to aim at in life: first to get what you want, and after that to enjoy it. Only the wisest achieve the second."

U.S. News and World Report confirms: "Once income provides basic needs, it doesn't correlate to happiness. Nor does intelligence, prestige or sunny weather. People grow used to better climates, higher salaries and newer cars."

And a report from the University of Southern California states: "Many of us are under the illusion that the more money we make, the happier we'll be. So we pour all our energies into making money and end up sacrificing our family and our health. The problem is, we don't realize that our material wants increase with the amount of money we make. The more we have, the more we seem to need."

After the residents of Grand Forks, North Dakota, were forced to abandon their homes to the rising river, they faced the daunting task of cleaning up. But while the flood ruined their homes, it didn't ruin their sense of humor. One homeowner placed a sign in his yard that read: "BASEMENT APARTMENT WITH INDOOR

POOL FOR RENT. JUST $20 A MONTH!" Another read: "WE KNOW WE'RE LUCKY, SO PLEASE STOP PRAYING FOR MORE GOOD FORTUNE!" However, an editorial in the local paper said it all:

"We are not what we own. If we were, we'd be far less than we were before the flood. The truth is, we are worth far more than our possessions. Our personal wealth does not indicate our personal worth."

Jesus said, "Life is not defined by what you have, even when you have a lot" (Lk 12:15 TM). Think about it: if money was the source of real happiness wouldn't the wealthy be less depressed than everybody else? They're not. Studies consistently show their happiness levels are just slightly above average—and in many cases far below. Despite what you may have been led to believe, happy people don't follow money, they follow something more lasting and satisfying—their God-given purpose in life!

Paul says, "Don't be obsessed with getting more material things" (Heb 13:5 TM). Often wealth-based status is a weakness indulged by insecure people who are afraid to look inside themselves. If you think money buys freedom, status or power—think again. The rich often become rich by sacrificing their freedom. And status is a slippery slope too, because no matter how far you climb there's always somebody further up the ladder. And worldly power? When that increases you can quickly lose control of your life because of all the people you have to please and the obligations you have to fulfill.

(2) Seeing pleasure as life's main course. Two cats were talking one day when one asked the other why he kept chasing his tail. "Well," he said, "My mom always told me happiness lies in your tail, so I'm trying to catch it." His friend replied, "But if you just kept walking wouldn't it follow you?" (Who said cats aren't smart?)

James writes, "Your motives are all wrong—

you want only what will give you pleasure" (Jas 4:3 NLT). When you overindulge in anything it loses its ability to satisfy. Wise people regularly back away from life's banquet so it stays fresh and fulfilling. On the other hand, pleasure-seekers and excitement-junkies dive in and wring every drop of gratification from it. But it doesn't work. It overloads the brain's pleasure centers, depletes the feel-good neurotransmitters, serotonin and dopamine, and fuels boredom, inflated expectations, and depression.

Paul said, "I've learned...to be...content whatever my circumstances...I've found the recipe for being happy...Whatever I have, wherever I am, I can make it through anything in the One who makes me who I am" (Php 4:11-13 TM).

The fact is, everybody dies, but not everybody really lives! Too many of us are having "near-life experiences." While money can buy options and creature comforts, the secret to lasting happiness is found by walking with God!

"Joyfulness is a learned skill.
You must take responsibility for your joy.
Not your friend, not your parent, not your
spouse, not your kids, not your boss—
your joy is your responsibility.
For some of us, this does not come easily,
you may be joy-impaired. You will have
to fight for it. But it can be done."

JOHN ORTBERG

CHAPTER NINE

Get Up and Keep Going!

In the Old Testament God told Joshua, "I have delivered Jericho into your hands, along with its king and its fighting men" (Jos 6:2 NIV). Notice He didn't say, "I will deliver," or "I might deliver." No. He said, "I *have* delivered." The city was already theirs, now they were being called to rise up and take possession of it.

God explained, "When you hear...the trumpets ...give a loud shout; then the wall of the city will collapse and [you] will go...straight in" (Jos 6:5 NIV). Now nobody in his right mind would expect a shout to bring down the walls of a big city. But this was no ordinary shout; it was a response to a promise made by God. You see faith isn't just believing God *can*, it's believing He *will* because

He keeps His promises. Initially there was no evidence of victory, but when Israel shouted God honored His Word and toppled the walls. When you're depressed the last thing you feel like doing is shouting, but you need to, and here's why:

(a) God has told you to. Paul says, "Merely hearing God's law is a waste of your time if you don't do what he commands. Doing...is what makes the difference" (Ro 2:13 TM). *(b) It confounds the enemy.* James writes, "Submit yourselves...to God. Resist the devil, and he will flee from you" (Jas 4:7). A life submitted to God is a Spirit-empowered life that wins out every time. *(c) Praise precedes victory.* When Israel went into battle Judah always led the way. The name Judah means, "Praise the Lord." Think: while they were praising God He was going ahead of them, dealing with their enemies.

Overcoming depression means constantly remembering:

(1) Every day is a gift. David said, "This is the

day which the Lord...made...we will rejoice and be glad in it" (Ps 118:24). Live each day like you won't be around tomorrow—for one day, perhaps sooner than you might think, that will be the case.

(2) Enjoy the little things in life. Some day you'll look back and realize they were the big things: like the glory of a sunset, your child's smile, the love of your family and friends, a walk in the park, good health. Feeling thankful and not expressing it is like wrapping a present and not giving it. Savor each moment. When you express appreciation for what you have, it multiplies!

(3) Stay positive. Peter McWilliams says, "There are two attorneys in your mind, one gathering evidence for 'Life is Awful,' the other for 'Life is Wonderful.' You are the judge; you can rule out any evidence you choose. So which ruling do you suppose will lead to joy and peace?"

At a café a woman was sitting near a family celebrating their son's basketball game. They were so excited she asked the boy, "Did your team win?"

Grinning from ear to ear he replied, "No, we lost by twenty points. We only made one basket." "Did you make it?" she asked. He shook his head, no. Just then his dad gave him a high-five and his Mom exclaimed, "You were awesome!" Seeing the woman's puzzled expression the boy explained, "Last game I took nine shots and all nine fell short of the basket. This game I took eight shots and three hit the rim. My dad says I'm making progress!" What an attitude!

Success isn't a destination; it's a journey. It's not just about winning, it's about growing. If you fail today, you get another chance tomorrow because God's "mercies begin afresh each morning" (Lam 3:23 NLT).

At the 1968 Mexico City Olympics a marathon runner wearing the colors of Tanzania limped into the station. His name was John Steven Aquari. His leg was bandaged because of an earlier fall. As he crossed the finish line far behind the others a spectator shouted, "Why didn't you just quit?" With quiet dignity Aquari replied, "My country didn't send me seven thousand miles to start this race—they sent me to finish it!"

Know what? God didn't send *you* to start this race either, He sent you to finish it! And He will encourage, equip and empower you to do it. You may be down but you're not out. Get up, dust yourself off and head for the finish line.

By God's grace you're going to make it!

A Prayer for Overcoming Depression

Lord, I come to You breaking under
the weight of this depression.
I can't carry it any longer.
So I lay it at Your feet and come into
agreement with Your Word, which says,
"I am the Lord that healeth thee."

Thank You for healing my mind,
my memories and my emotions.
Thank you for lifting me out of depression,
for helping me to walk in the joy You give
day by day. You came to set the captive free.
Today, I choose to walk in that freedom
and be made whole.

In Jesus' Name...
Amen.

Acknowledgments

Meyer, Joyce. *Straight Talk on Depression.* (Warner Books, Fenton, Miss. 1998)

Armentrout, David P. *Heart Cry! God's Prescription for Depression.* (Ragged Edge Press, Shippenburg, Pa.)

Sutton, Mark A. and Hennigan, Bruce M.D. *Conquering Depression.* (Broadman & Holman Publishers, Nashville, Tenn. 2001)

Gass, Bob. *Help! I'm Depressed.* (Celebration Enterprises, Roswell, Ga. 2002)

Clark, Warren Neil. *God Said It, Don't Sweat It.* (Thomas Nelson, Nashville, Tenn. 1998)

Lucado, Max. *The Applause of Heaven.* (W. Publishing Group, Nashville, Tenn.)

Lucado, Max. *Next Door Savior.* (W. Publishing Group, Nashville, Tenn. 2003)

Lucado, Max. *He Still Moves Stones.* (W. Publishing Group Nashville, Tenn. 2003)

Blackaby, Richard and Henry. *Experiencing God Day by Day.* (Broadman & Holman, Nashville, Tenn. 1998)

Ortberg, John. *Everybody's Normal Till You Get to Know Them.* (Zondervan, Grand Rapids, Mich. 2003)

Waldman, Jackie. *The Courage to Give.* (Conari Press)

McDowell, Josh. *See Yourself as God Sees You.* (Tyndale House, Wheaton, Ill. 1999)

Ortberg, John. *If You Want to Walk on Water You've Got to Get Out of the Boat.* (Zondervan Publishing, Grand Rapids, Mich. 2005)

Breathnach, Sarah Ban. *Romancing the Ordinary.* (Simple Abundance Press, New York, N.Y.)

Baker, Dan Ph.D., and Stauth, Cameron. *What Happy People Know: How the New Science of Happiness Can Change Your Life for the Better.* (Rodale Press)

Bombeck, Erma. *If Life Is a Bowl of Cherries, What Am I Doing in the Pits?* (Ballantine Books, Inc. 1979)